the Spirit of Racing

The Spirit of Racing

KENSINGTON WEST PRODUCTIONS

HEXHAM ENGLAND

Kensington West Productions Ltd
5 Cattle Market, Hexham, Northumberland NE46 1NJ
Tel: (01434) 609933, Fax: (01434) 600066

Photographs by
Trevor Jones and George Selwyn

Editors
Julian West, Barry Roxburgh

Editorial Contributor
Karen Ryan

Designed by
Diane Ridley

Production
Mark Scandle

Origination by
Pre-Press Ltd, Hong Kong

Printing by
Midas Printing Ltd, Hong Kong

Special thanks to Gill Jones for her hours of hard work and encouragement and Mike Allen of "Fixation" in London for faultless support of the Nikon camera system

Frontispiece: **Hooves at Lingfield Photograph by George Selwyn**

Title Page: **Parade Ring on the July Course Photograph by Trevor Jones**
Facing: **Tony McCoy a heavy fall at Cheltenham Photograph by George Selwyn**

Acknowledgements: **The Grand Prix at St Moritz (above) Photograph by Trevor Jones**
In the pool at Al Quoz, Dubai (below) Photograph by Trevor Jones
A long walk home at Cheltenham (facing) Phtotograph by Trevor Jones

Contents: **At the Start, Sandown (above and below) Photographs by George Selwyn**

Contents

Introduction

by Brough Scott

More than a sport? Those in doubt should take a look. Racing can be a vocation, an addiction, a heritage and a business all in one. Racing pictures should always be about a lot more than just the racecourse.

That's why it is so good to browse around a book like this. Its images remind you of the layers of pleasure and interest that the racing fan can find. Everyone will share in the punch-the-air thrill of a Dettori victory on the racetrack. But everyone should also revel in the timeless peace of mares and foals in the paddocks. For within a couple of years those youngsters will themselves be out carrying your money while the whips crack and the bookies roar.

In many ways the paddock is the place to start. On a summer morning with just birdsong and bee hum for company you need to pinch yourself to think that these frisking sets of cheek on legs are what much of this whole gloriously absurd circus is all about. That these foals are a direct result of a process set in train a full three centuries ago. That this thoroughbred, this breed, has been England's greatest gift to the animal kingdom and is the same breed you will find on racetracks in America, Japan, Australia, Argentina and all places east and west.

But when you stand there with the sun on your back and the grasslands in front it is easy to lapse into an image of Eden before Adam came (and of course Eve wasn't far behind). To think how much happier racing would be if it were only about horses and did not have man to mess it up.

Yet that is to yearn for a useless unrealistic idyll. It is only because of the man on his back that the racehorse actually knows where to race. What's more—and if we harp back to that original Eden this is where the serpent came in—it is only because of the betting snake that every outsider can get truly involved, rather than being just a distant fan. He or she can test their wits at trying to make the galloping jigsaw fit. They can put their money down. They can win and lose. They can find their share of happiness, and of wickedness too.

In that way the game quickly becomes so much more than a sport. It is a whole kaleidoscope of locations and emotions that go from little track to large, from labourer to plutocrat, from floodlit desert nights to rainswept Cotswold hills, from bright eyed kids to purple faced pensioners, from true heroics to the shifty corruption that always lurks.

Yes, more than any other sporting activity, racing can hook you from the cradle to the grave.

Because of this there has never been an easy way to put a caption on it. So often racing's diverse parts descend into mutual distrust. The celebration of one section frequently chooses to ignore or disparage the achievements of another part of the game's many sides. That is why it is so good to be reminded of what an all-encompassing passion this whole thing can be. Why the Spirit of Racing should be welcomed wherever a racing eye can see.

Trainer Henry Cecil contemplates on Warren Hill (above).
Selling Ring, Windsor (opposite).

Photographs by George Selwyn

Chapter One

Beginnings & Endings

The dawn of a new day. New hopes and new chances to win. The pattern is repeated every twenty four hours around the world.

Sunrise at Santa Anita (facing left)
Nicky Henderson's first lot on a crisp Lambourn morning (above)

PHOTOGRAPHS BY TREVOR JONES

Stallions provide the lifeblood for a new generation of equine heroes. Their racing days now over, they begin their new career at stud as masters of the harem.

Wolfhound at Dalham Hall Stud, Newmarket (above facing).
French champion Nureyev at Walmac Stud, Lexington, Kentucky (below facing).
US Grade 1 winner AP Indy (below).

PHOTOGRAPHS BY TREVOR JONES (above facing and below)
PHOTOGRAPH BY GEORGE SELWYN (below facing)

While many might think winning a million for a race is a king's ransom, it can be but a drop in the ocean compared with the financial rewards of owning a successful stallion. Little wonder that they live a life of luxury.

Dalham Hall Stud, Newmarket (opposite).
French stallion Lead on Time at Haras du Quesnay Stud, Deauville (above).

PHOTOGRAPH BY TREVOR JONES (opposite)
PHOTOGRAPH BY GEORGE SELWYN (above)

Eating up: a vital sign of the health of any thoroughbred. No problems in this regard for French Derby winner Old Vic and Group One winner Pivotal.

Pivotal (left).
Pivotal at Cheveley Park Stud, Newmarket (below).
Old Vic at Dalham Hall Stud, Newmarket (opposite).

PHOTOGRAPHS BY TREVOR JONES

Celtic Swing at the National Stud, Newmarket (above).
Cadeaux Genereux at Whitsbury Manor Stud, Hampshire (opposite).

PHOTOGRAPHS BY TREVOR JONES

Dalham Hall's stallion Mark of Esteem scenting. The quest for the perfect foal begins. But which stallion and which mare? The time honoured conundrum for breeders throughout the world.

Mark of Esteem at Dalham Hall Stud.

PHOTOGRAPH BY TREVOR JONES

Mare and foal at Dalham Hall Stud, Newmarket.

<small>Photograph by George Selwyn</small>

Champion sprinter Lochsong at Littleton Stud, Hampshire.

PHOTOGRAPH BY TREVOR JONES

Foal at Stetchworth Park Stud, Newmarket (above).
Zafonic at Banstead Manor Stud, Newmarket (right).

PHOTOGRAPHS BY TREVOR JONES

Breeding

by Julian Muscat

Racecourses are places of genuine excitement. Even the uninitiated can sense the joy, the passion, the sheer love of horses that radiates from a knowledgeable crowd. Nevertheless, those intent on touching the soul of the sport must look elsewhere. The essence of the thoroughbred, and what it truly represents, can be found on the nation's pastures. It is where fledgling racehorses are born and reared - in harness with the dreams of their creators.

Watch any owner pace the paddock and you will identify his profound excitement. Watch any breeder welcome a newborn into the world and you will identify a different sensation. The foals are their children—they must be nursed, educated and prepared for the day when they leave home to embark on life's great adventure. What you see on the racecourse—a strapping, shining thoroughbred—is largely the result of two years' intense preparation by that horse's breeder.

Two years is no time at all. Indeed, it is startling to behold that a newborn foal, its legs seemingly as frail as a spider's, will soon be pounding the racecourse, its back laden with 9st of jockey, saddle and lead. Of course, no amount of money and personal attention can enhance a horse's speed. That is entirely in the hands of nature, who bestows her gifts with random abandon. If disappointment invariably prevails over unbroken success, it is what makes the pursuit worthwhile. As you watch a herd of foals cavorting through the paddocks, who is to say the little chestnut will not win a Group race ? Or the striking bay with the four white socks ?

Within the confines of this uncertainty lies an element of natural selection - itself the raison d' être behind all existing species in the wild. It follows that a product of champion thoroughbreds is more likely to succeed than one from ordinary performers. However, the margins are minuscule - which is why there is always a hope. The breed needs champions from previously undistinguished lineage to ensure its vigour and strength. While Middle Eastern gentlemen invest fortunes in patronising the best stallions, they could one day be beating a path to your door, anxious to secure some of the lines you have cultivated from unpromising origins.

Expectation is the byword but there is a resonance in failure. Captain Tim Forster, the National Hunt trainer and arch-pessimist, has plundered countless top steeplechases. His expression rarely changes until he recounts the breeding disasters endured by his owner/ breeders down the decades. He speaks of stillborn foals, of legs like glass, of tendons bowed like bananas..... and then he smiles and says : "That is why you genuinely appreciate the good ones when they come along." It also explains why Forster hates watching his horses compete, for fear of another calamitous injury.

There are endless sporting projects through which one can sift one's wealth. Breeding racehorses is among the most costly, although none is more enjoyable. Each day you can cast your eye across open fields, watching a mare and her sibling in as natural a habitat as thoroughbreds will ever encounter. You can identify their traits, their temperament, their foibles, their dislikes. And when it is time for them to pass into the racing world, you have next year's crop to ease the sense of loss. The time will have come to start again.

The innocence of youth and the quiet beauty of mother and child.
Carefree for now; if only it would always be this way.

Indian Skimmer and her foal (above).
Foal in a field at Dalham Hall Stud (opposite).

PHOTOGRAPH BY GEORGE SELWYN (above)
PHOTOGRAPH BY TREVOR JONES (opposite)

*W*hat a vendor, but what a buy. The ratatatat auctioneering at Tattersalls - masters of their profession.
Bosra Sham- expensive, yes - but what value. Henry Cecil's greatest ever, now <u>that</u> really is something.

Auctioneer David Pim (above left).
Bosra Sham goes into the auction ring (above right).

PHOTOGRAPHS BY TREVOR JONES

*W*ho's bidding? Who's buying? What's the price? What's
the currency? It used to be Lire, but now it's Yen.

Buyers at Tattersalls, Newmarket (above).
Bids in different currencies (left).

PHOTOGRAPH BY GEORGE SELWYN (above)
PHOTOGRAPH BY TREVOR JONES (left)

Rags or riches? *"The horse is ours at a great price...just wait until next year when we get him to the races."*

Tattersalls Sales (opposite).
Leaving the sale ring at Tattersalls (above).
Lots board at Tattersalls (right).

PHOTOGRAPH BY GEORGE SELWYN (opposite and right)
PHOTOGRAPH BY TREVOR JONES (above)

*T*raining: Like humans, some horses are easier to train than others.
But with everything to play for, education is crucial to success.

In Training

PHOTOGRAPH BY TREVOR JONES

An upset in the parade ring...

Sandown Parade Ring

PHOTOGRAPH BY GEORGE SELWYN

... going to post ...

Going to Post at York

PHOTOGRAPH BY GEORGE SELWYN

... or at the start can cost a good horse the race.

At the Start

PHOTOGRAPH BY GEORGE SELWYN

Lest we forget. Former champions of the Turf.
They came, they saw, they conquered.

Bronze of Gladiateur, Longchamp (top left).
Red Rum's bronze at Aintree (middle left).
Statue of Mill Reef at the National Stud,
Newmarket (bottom left).
Winning silks from Dettori's magnificent
seven in the Horseracing Museum,
Newmarket (above).
Statue of Dawn Run and Jonjo O'Neill at
Cheltenham (opposite).

PHOTOGRAPHS BY TREVOR JONES (top left, bottom
left , above and opposite)
PHOTOGRAPH BY GEORGE SELWYN (middle left)

Training at Hollywood Park, California (above).
Horses after exercise at Whatcombe (opposite).

PHOTOGRAPH BY GEORGE SELWYN (above)
PHOTOGRAPH BY TREVOR JONES (opposite)

Chapter Two

Behind the Scenes

Keeping it in the family: Ed Dunlop will have picked up more than a useful tip or two from his distinguished father John.

Horse in training at Ed Dunlop's yard (left). **John Dunlop checking his horses on returning from training** (below).

PHOTOGRAPH BY TREVOR JONES (left)
PHOTOGRAPH BY GEORGE SELWYN (below)

The Peaks and Troughs of Training

by John Karter

Who'd be a racehorse trainer? Fêted by princes, peers and sheikhs, partying with the rich and famous, driving to the races in shiny BMWs and Mercs, jetting off to racetracks round the world. It's a dirty job but somebody's got to do it.

The "silver spoon" perception of a trainer's lot arguably fits many people's notion of the way life really is in Newmarket, Lambourn and Epsom—fun and games and a licence to print money to boot. As with so many things in this topsy-turvy world, reality and fantasy are very different.

Depending on which particular trainer or trainers you base your perception upon, it might indeed be easy to regard them as well-heeled hedonists. Then again, if you look further down the ladder, it would be equally possible to see them as certifiable lunatics, putting themselves through an endless cycle of hard work and heartache while the overdraft gets bigger by the day.

One thing is beyond question. Whether you are top dog with 200 blue-blooded throughbreds peeping out from behind your stable doors or a struggling West Country licence holder with a yard full of cheapies and cast-offs, training is a profession that obliges you to be all things to all men.

The modern trainer must combine the qualities of managing director, veterinarian, accountant and public relations expert. He must have the ability to make endless small talk with owners from all walks of life, and an unquenchable (should that be warped?) sense of humour. He must also possess the physical and mental energy of a 20-year-old, incredible resilience, and skin as thick as a warthog's. For all this he can expect to work not less than 16 hours per day, seven days a week, with an income that fluctuates as wildly as the form of the average racehorse.

Such matters are of minor consequence. When it all comes together training must surely be one of the most satisfying forms of eking out a living known to man. If you have ever been up on Newmarket Heath or Lambourn or Epsom Downs as the first fingers of dawn reach out across a dappled summer sky and watched spellbound as a trainer puts his team of glistening equine athletes through their paces you will know that this is racing's version of nirvana.

Morning exercise, with racehorses skimming across the skyline and work riders poised hawk-like on their backs, is truly a timeless scene that can engender an almost primitive excitement in aficiionado and first-timer alike. Clive Brittain, the successful Newmarket trainer, summed it up perfectly when he said: "You go out there in the morning and it's like an oil painting. But while an Old Master stays the same, the racing scene is always changing."

An ever-changing cast of equine players ensures the constant development–and therein lies the answer to the ultimate question. The spur that keeps trainers motivated, even when they have hit rock bottom, is the unyielding hope that lurking among the latest intake of spindly-legged youngsters is the outstanding individual, the embryo Classic winner, possibly even the international champion, that will make all the hard times worthwhile.

Could there be anything more satisfying than watching that raw, uncoordinated yearling you instinctively believed in gallop to victory in a prestigious race at Epsom or Ascot? For someone who operates at much less rarifed levels, winning the humblest selling race can be as satisfying as lifting a Derby or Grand National.

Yet even when you have finally unearthed the pearl it can be dashed cruelly from your grasp. Thoroughbreds are the most delicate creatures both in terms of constitiution and physique. When you have honed your stable star to perfection, disaster can strike at the very moment when you should be reaching out for glorious victory.

Nicky Henderson, a leading National Hunt trainer, put it this way. "When the Good Lord made racehorses he didn't intend clowns like us to handle them, otherwise he would have made them out of steel not china."

So, it is not all wine and roses, but it is certainly not all sackcloth and ashes either. Yes, there are appalling troughs that can bring strong men to their knees, but then there are the magniificent, soaring peaks. They are something only those masochistic "clowns" who call themselves trainers could possibly explain.

Expectancy. Where are we going today, Guv'nor? Light work? The Races? Or just hanging around here? Horses await the day's orders at Toby Balding's yard, while on the Newmarket gallops a young apprentice (Frankie Dettori) puts another star of the future through his paces.

Toby Balding's yard (left).
Apprentice Dettori rides work (right).

PHOTOGRAPHS BY TREVOR JONES

5:30 am. Dressed for work? Top Flat and National Hunt trainer
Mary Reveley offers an early morning snack to one of her charges.
6:30 am. At Belmont Park dawn breaks a little later as thoroughbred
cars and horses prepare for the day.

Trainer Mary Reveley feeding at 5:30 am (facing).
Belmont Park, New York (above).

PHOTOGRAPHS BY GEORGE SELWYN

Divine intuition? Is he fit? Is he sound? Is he ready to win a Classic? Mister Baileys leads the string out of Mark Johnston's yard for a piece of work. The answer: He's fit, he's well and he wins the 2000 Guineas.

Mister Baileys wins the 1994 Guineas from Grand Lodge (above).
Mister Baileys leads the string out of Mark Johnston's Middleham yard (left).

PHOTOGRAPHS BY TREVOR JONES

Newmarket: Britain's racing headquarters has the busiest gallops in the world. On a fine day there is probably no better place to be.

Training at Newmarket

PHOTOGRAPH BY TREVOR JONES

Not so hard please! A bit behind the ears will do nicely. Bayakoa gets an early morning wipe down after work at Florida's Gulfstream Park. At Miho training centre in Japan a similar scene is enacted.

Bayakoa at Gulfstream Park, Florida (left).
Miho Training Centre, Japan (right facing).

PHOTOGRAPHS BY GEORGE SELWYN

*L*ords of the Manor. A classic morning scene at Charlie Brooks's Lambourn yard. Another of Britain's racing heartlands where training horses paints a permanent picture on an ever-changing landscape.

Horses at Charlie Brooks's yard, Lambourn (opposite).
Lambourn Gallops (above).

PHOTOGRAPHS BY TREVOR JONES

Dreams are made of this. Two year olds at Manton, where Peter Chapple-Hyam trains with considerable success for Robert Sangster.

Two year olds at Manton.

PHOTOGRAPH BY GEORGE SELWYN

Ballydoyle in Ireland. The former kingdom of legendary trainer Vincent O'Brien,
the gallops are now home to namesake Aidan, who has assumed the mantle with dramatic success.

Ballydoyle all-weather gallops.

PHOTOGRAPH BY GEORGE SELWYN

No rest for the wicked. Newmarket's celebrated Warren Hill - the town beats to the sound of horses' hooves.
A nonchalant lad at French trainer Andre Fabre's yard goes about his daily routine.

Newmarket's Warren Hill (left).
Andre Fabre's yard, Chantilly (right).

PHOTOGRAPH BY TREVOR JONES (left)
PHOTOGRAPH BY GEORGE SELWYN (right)

Come on in - the water's lovely. The therapy of swimming is as well known around the world as Newmarket trainer Clive Brittain's outstanding success in farming top international races.

Exercise in Clive Brittain's equine pool, Newmarket (above and right).

<small>PHOTOGRAPHS BY TREVOR JONES</small>

Sun, sea and sand. Salt water invigorates in a spin along Deauville's beach on the French coast. On Ireland's Laytown beach horse and horseman carve out a circular course in the sand.

On the beach at Deauville (above).
On the beach at Laytown, County Meath (left).

PHOTOGRAPHS BY TREVOR JONES

All in a day's work. Whether you're called an American blacksmith or an English farrier, your work is an essential part of the racing scene...

Blacksmith at Hollywood Park, California (left).
The English Farrier (below).

PHOTOGRAPH BY GEORGE SELWYN (LEFT).
PHOTOGRAPH BY TREVOR JONES (BELOW)

Town meets country and seaside on the training grounds of trainer Mary Reveley's Saltburn gallops on England's North East coast.

Training at Mary Reveley's Saltburn yard (opposite).

PHOTOGRAPH BY GEORGE SELWYN

...as are saddle makers and the ever present stable lads and trainers, whether mucking out or riding out.

Covered ride at John Gosden's Stanley House Stables, Newmarket (above).
Saddle maker at Lindsay Park Stud, Australia (top right).
John Berry mucks out, Newmarket (bottom right).

PHOTOGRAPH BY TREVOR JONES (above)
PHOTOGRAPHS BY GEORGE SELWYN (top right and bottom right)

A penny for your thoughts Mr Cecil. One of the game's training greats in deep contemplation as he leads his hack Impressario homeward.

Henry Cecil 1993.

PHOTOGRAPH BY TREVOR JONES

Lucky for some. A black cat at Hollywood Park gives his blessing to an equine neighbour. Horseshoes are always a symbol of good luck.

Former jumping great Remittance Man always travelled with his own good luck charm and faithful companion, Nobby the sheep.

Morning at Hollywood Park, California (above).
Racing shoe (left).
Remittance Man and friend Nobby the sheep (opposite).

PHOTOGRAPHS BY GEORGE SELWYN (above and left)
PHOTOGRAPH BY TREVOR JONES (opposite)

A *world apart. The morning sun welcomes a new day for trainer Satish Seemar at the Zabeel Stables in Dubai's desert...*

...while trainer David Elsworth ponders another bright future for his stable stars amidst the winter snow.

David Elsworth's string at Whitsbury (below).
Zabeel Stables, Dubai (right).
UAE Trainer Satish Seemar (facing).

PHOTOGRAPHS BY TREVOR JONES (right and facing)
PHOTOGRAPH BY GEORGE SELWYN (below)

Over a Railway fence at Sandown Park (above).
Cheltenham spectators (opposite).

PHOTOGRAPH BY GEORGE SELWYN (above)
PHOTOGRAPH BY TREVOR JONES (opposite)

Chapter Three

At the Races

An exhausted and disconsolate Michael Roberts after a race at Sandown Park. The race is over for jockey Robert Bellamy after parting company with his mount New Halen at the 19th fence in the Grand National. Black Tie Affair lifts the world's richest race, of 1991 the Breeders' Cup Classic at Churchill Downs.

Michael Roberts (above).
Robert Bellamy (left).
Black Tie Affair (facing).

PHOTOGRAPHS BY GEORGE SELWYN

*They're off! Hopes are high as tons of thoroughbred muscle leap for the stars at Kempton Park.
Binoculars raised at the punters' extravaganza, the National Hunt Festival at Cheltenham.*

Kempton Park (left)
Cheltenham crowds (above)

PHOTOGRAPHS BY TREVOR JONES

Summer thrills or winter spills. Two of the finest sights in racing. The anticipation of a fiercely contested hurdle race at Cheltenham and York's picture book parade ring at August's Ebor meeting.

Cheltenham (left).
York's Parade Ring (right).

PHOTOGRAPHS BY TREVOR JONES

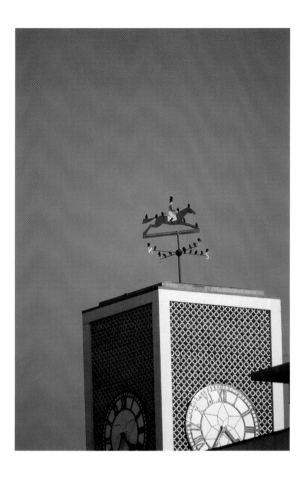

Ascot's weather vane is kind. Jockeys take their roll call for the starter's fierce growl. Meanwhile the tic tac man's gesture relays a different message.

Tic Tac man (left).
Ascot's weather vane (above left).
Starter (above centre).
Raceboard (above right).

PHOTOGRAPHS BY TREVOR JONES

A word in your ear my friend and I can't hear a thing with these mufflers. Ears pricked as the protagonists make their way to the start on opposite sides of the world—Fuchi, Japan and York's Knavesmire.

Japan (above).
York (right).

PHOTOGRAPHS BY GEORGE SELWYN

Do we bow now or after the race? Jockeys at Tokyo's racecourse wait to saddle up. The scene of enduring formality takes a different twist at Cheltenham as riders show their mounts the first of many fences.

Tokyo (top right).
Cheltenham (bottom right).

PHOTOGRAPHS BY TREVOR JONES

Inspecting the form book at Newmarket (above left).
Punters and their form in Japan (above right).
Studying the card at Royal Ascot (right).

PHOTOGRAPHS BY GEORGE SELWYN

*T*he vain pursuit of finding winners. Racecards, newspapers, form books, all endeavour to provide the vital clue...this pastime absorbs some more than others.

Racegoers at Royal Ascot (above).

PHOTOGRAPH BY TREVOR JONES

Gallic stoicism meets Ascot joie de vivre - all men are equal on the turf and six feet under it, or so the saying goes.

Meanwhile, another racing adage is that it's all about a piece of wood - the winning post of the Epsom Derby. Seldom has a Derby been so hard fought as the piece of wood comes just in time for Benny the Dip.

Royal Ascot (above).
Crowd, Saint Cloud (right).
Benny the Dip (facing).

PHOTOGRAPHS BY GEORGE SELWYN

The regal tradition of Royal Ascot—multi-million pound horsepower on the hoof as well as behind the Grandstand.

Procession of carriages from Windsor Castle (above).
Horseless carriages await the Royal departure. (below).
The winner's enclosure (right).

PHOTOGRAPHS BY TREVOR JONES

In France, Longchamp's moulin and Chantilly's chateau are fit for a king's horses as well as his men.

Longchamp (right), **Chantilly** (left).

PHOTOGRAPHS BY TREVOR JONES

*T*he sublime south downs of Sussex and Glorious Goodwood. A typical leisurely gallop through the fields for the Festival Stakes is brought to breakneck reality in a hard fought finish to the Stewards Cup sprint.

Festival Stakes (right).
Stewards Cup (above).

PHOTOGRAPHS BY TREVOR JONES

Flat Racing

by Julian West

Flat racing's enduring fascination lies in its variety. Distances, courses, surfaces, weather and going conditions all contribute to why form is so difficult to fathom and use to beat the odds. With the advent of truly international racing over the past decade, this has never been more the case. Jockeys, trainers, horses and connections now travel the world in search of the glory and the cash to finance even more glorious victories.

But how do you compare the achievements of one horse in March on Dubai sand, with the same horse's possibilities in the Arc on soft going in October? If flat racing was played out on a truly level playing field it would be difficult enough. But how do you compare Goodwood's undulations with Belmont's long sweeping dirt straight? Just when you think you may have an insight into the permutation, along comes a European classic winner entered for a handicap in the southern hemisphere at the wrong time of year and probably over the wrong distance in the greatest distance handicap of them all, the Melbourne Cup.

The money's there though for those who venture to be brave. Never before have the prizes been so glittering on the course and off it and in the breeding game. An English Derby winner going to stud in Japan is not front page news any more. Money talks like it never did before.

No, it's not an easy game this, and hats off to the connections and trainers who make it all possible, and the jockeys, for whom success is now a worldwide quest. What other sport in the world would ask its heroes to perform over the minimum distance of five eighths of a mile one moment and to ride with accurate pace in a race over four times as long on a different animal a mere thirty minutes later. OK Pete Sampras, you've won a grand slam. How about it if we change the rules a bit and make the court four times as big the next time?

No, the four seasons of racing now demand complete and utter dedication to the game. They say it's a young man's game at that, but where are the Piggotts and Shoemakers of other sports? How many other people in other sports make a comeback in something as physically demanding as flat racing in their late fifties?

The case for the defence rests. From Salisbury to Sha Tin, from Churchill Downs to Catterick. Bring on the next season with its infinite wonder and the next generation of three year olds to gaze at, gleaming in the parade ring, and suppose if three to one is the right price.

The Sport of Kings may have lost a few crowned heads over the years, but the title still holds true. And whether you're loftily placed from birth, or prefer to watch the horses go down from the public enclosure, you will always have the chance to say "I saw a future champion today and I can follow him to the ends of the earth".

*L*ife's a beach! *Children of all ages take it easy at the races.*
While one cools down with an ice cream, another warms up with
his own sprint.

Chantilly classic scene (above).
Parasols on parade, Deauville (right).
A hot day at Chantilly sur l'herbe (facing top).
Cooling breezes at the Laytown Races (facing bottom).

PHOTOGRAPHS BY TREVOR JONES

When the tide goes out. Churchill Down's dirt track after a heavy shower does its own imitation of Laytown's beach. *The swings and roundabouts of racing life.*

Churchill Downs, Kentucky (facing).
Beach course at Laytown, County Meath (above).
Swings at Laytown (right).

PHOTOGRAPHS BY TREVOR JONES.

Country racing in France has its own quiet pleasures. The ultimate winner leads the field in the Grand Steeplechase at Granville. The number board reveals some late withdrawals. Was it the hard ground?

Granville, France. Jumping the 7th from home (winner inside) (right).
Number board at Granville (above).

<small>Photographs by George Selwyn</small>

The ups and downs of racing. Turning for home at Cheltenham with a double handful at your disposal. Far from the madding crowd remounting sometimes makes the best of a long trip home.

Cheltenham (above).
After the Fall (left and right).

PHOTOGRAPHS BY TREVOR JONES

National Hunt Racing

by Alastair Down

There is something slightly unhinged and mildly obsessive about jump racing fans. They are the type of people who wouldn't go to Royal Ascot if it was held in their back garden, but would walk barefoot across a mile of fakir's beds for a day at Ludlow or Fontwell. Unlike flat racing, jumping has a soul. There is such a thing as the "Spirit of National Hunt Racing" and the flame of that spirit burns unquenchable.

In these days of central heating, cars with climate control and outdoor clothing that would keep you warm in the Arctic, an afternoon's jump racing offers one of the last chances to get totally and irredeemably frozen to the marrow. If there is a colder place to be than the centre of the course at Wetherby as a January gale blows in from the North East, I have yet to find it.

Yet the beauty of jump racing is that even when you are both terminally hypothermic and unquestionably skint, the action suddenly reaches out and recharges the spirit. Whereas bad flat racing is only ever bad flat racing, I have seen some chronically slow old selling chaser at Plumpton dig deep for victory and paint a big smile across the faces of the hardy souls on hand to witness it.

Part of the game's appeal is that it is a true democracy. Some city fat cat might spend fortunes on the finest prospects money can buy, yet when push comes to shove in the run from the last fence, his pride and joy can still get run out of it by some local farmer's yak that was bred at home and spends its days rounding up sheep on the fell. For the racegoer and punter, there is a strong degree of admiration for those horses and the bunch of one-offs who ride them for a living.

We all know just how randomly dangerous the sport is and that quite suddenly and with chilling finality such minor issues as victory and defeat can be put in perspective by death or serious injury. Love of the sport is very closely informed by an outspoken acknowledgement of the risks being run by man and beast in order to offer us matchless entertainment.

Unlike other sports, the racing faithful are not there to support clubs, teams or countries, they are drawn there by the picture as a whole, not some factional loyalty to part of it. Of course we form our affections and cleave wholeheartedly to them. The great jump stars shine in the sporting firmament for year after year–they become valued friends and part of the furniture of one's experience.

Just occasionally a horse will transcend the limits of the sport and leap into a wider public prominence. In my lifetime Arkle, Red Rum and Desert Orchid have all become heroes to a section of the populace to whom Towcester is something to put bread in and The Chair is a place to sit. But these great household name horses, whose brilliance and courage outgrew the confines of National Hunt Racing, are mirrored further down the scale by countless horses that the racing public become attached to.

Jumping and jump horses get under your skin and wheedle their way into your affections. However unsentimental you try to be about animals, some of the so-and-so's get you in the end. Their extraordinary guts in battling up the hill at Cheltenham simply demands your emotional involvement in return. If a race like Dawn Run's Gold Cup fails to move you, then you have mislaid the capacity to be moved.

As a child my hero in racing was a gritty old chaser called Rondetto. He won the Hennessy in 1968 but his main claim to fame was the number of times he kept failing to win the Grand National. If anything could go wrong at Aintree it did. He was the only horse to jump the 23rd other than Foinavon in 1967, only to unseat his rider on landing. He fell when cantering another year and was also brought down when storming along up with the leaders on another occasion. Finally in 1969, at the age of 14, he got round to finish the most honourable of thirds and to a small boy one year younger than Rondetto this was the answer to many prayers and the greatest of thrills. Watching television at home, that 13 year old wept happy tears that his old hero had finally earned some of his just deserts round that most fearsome of courses.

It is now 28 years since that afternoon. I am older, tougher and much more cynical, but I am glad to say I couldn't promise not to do the same if circumstances repeated themselves. If you are tired of this game, or it ceases to touch you, you are indeed tired of life.

*R*acing on the All Weather and in all weathers. From Santa Anita's palm fringed bowl to a not-so-leafy Lingfield Park in winter. But Lingfield gets its share of blue skies at other times of the year.

Santa Anita (right).
Lingfield Park (facing above and below).

PHOTOGRAPHS BY TREVOR JONES

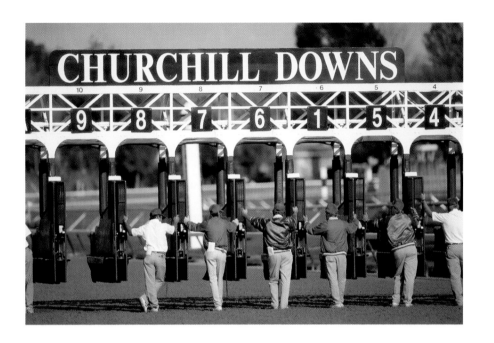

The foggy start of a National Hunt race at Ascot paints a classic picture of the British winter game. At Churchill Downs in Kentucky stalls handlers adopt a languid pose before racing explodes into action.

Ascot fog (far left).
Kentucky start (top and bottom left).

PHOTOGRAPH BY GEORGE SELWYN (far left)
PHOTOGRAPHS BY TREVOR JONES (Top and bottom left)

Attempted starts, aborted starts and in full flight. Drama at the post of the Aintree Grand National that never was in 1993. A less serious moment perhaps as a rider is dumped to the turf at the start of the Sun Alliance Chase at Cheltenham. Once they're off though its all thrills and spills over the National course's Becher's Brook.

Cheltenham start (top).
National false start (bottom)
Becher's Brook (facing).

PHOTOGRAPH BY TREVOR JONES (top)
PHOTOGRAPHS BY GEORGE SELWYN
(bottom and facing)

Tops and tails and fairy tales. The grey Morcelli embarks upon a copybook leap while jockeys at Cheltenham and Aintree ponder their sad or happy endings.

Aintree heads (top left).
Cheltenham tails (bottom left).
Morcelli (facing).

PHOTOGRAPHS BY TREVOR JONES
(top and bottom left)
PHOTOGRAPH BY GEORGE SELWYN
(facing)

*T*wo of the great National Hunt jockeys pay for the error of their ways - Dunwoody and Francome hit the deck, while Cavvies Clown finds his own way through the fence. Novice chasers at Leicester, negotiating the water at Doncaster and four out of five show text book form at Cheltenham.

Richard Dunwoody fall (top left), **Cavvies Clown** (middle left). **Five in line at Cheltenham** (facing). **Doncaster water jump** (above top), **Leicester novice chase** (above) **and John Francome fall** (bottom left).

PHOTOS BY TREVOR JONES (top left, middle left and facing)
PHOTOS BY GEORGE SELWYN (bottom left, above top and above)

You're nicked! Eagle eyed stewards at the Curragh. A disqualification in progress in Ascot's Bessborough Stakes when Vouchsafe is later denied the first prize for interference. At Aintree the long arm of the law makes further arrests.

Aintree Police (facing).
Stewards at the Curragh (above).
Bessborough Stakes (left and above top).

PHOTOGRAPHS BY GEORGE SELWYN

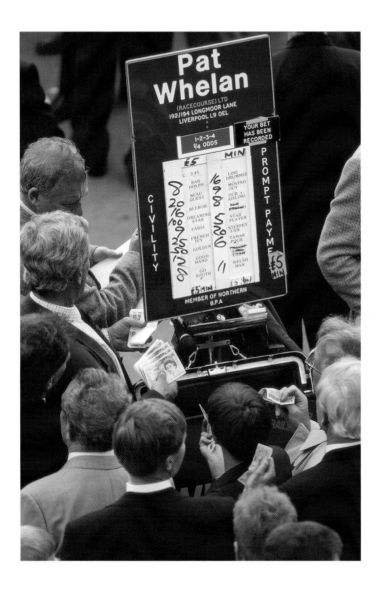

Some bookmakers have a better view than others. Goodwood's Trundle Hill offers more view than action while Pat Whelan has less view but presumably more profit.

Goodwood's Trundle Hill (above.)
Bookies at the course (left).

PHOTOGRAPHS BY TREVOR JONES.

Packing them in at the betting jungle (below).
Rails bookmakers deal across the great divide at Cheltenham (right).

PHOTOGRAPHS BY TREVOR JONES

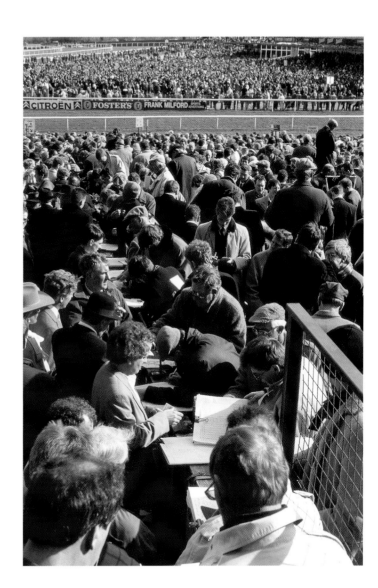

In England's green and pleasant land.

Goodwood's two mile start paints a Degas scene (top).
Runners return at Chester (left).
Saddling up in the parade ring on Newmarket's July course (facing).

PHOTOGRAPHS BY TREVOR JONES

An Australian trainer shows the latest in outback fashion. The unique windmill whip style of the Aussie jockey would land him in deep water in Pommie land.

Doing it Down Under (left and below).
Flemington Racecourse isn't really for the birds (facing).

PHOTOGRAPHS BY GEORGE SELWYN

The Dubai World Cup is the richest prize in international racing's present pantheon of glittering trophies.

All that glitters is gold (facing).
It never rains but it pours, even in the desert (below).

PHOTOGRAPH BY GEORGE SELWYN (below)
PHOTOGRAPH BY TREVOR JONES (facing)

Big city lights. The crowds pack in and the betting pools soar as high as the skyscrapers in Hong Kong by day and night.

Night racing at Happy Valley (above).
Down the back straight at Sha Tin (facing).

PHOTOGRAPHS BY GEORGE SELWYN

Tomorrow is another day - the last race at a summer evening meeting at Newmarket.

Last race at Newmarket (above).

PHOTOGRAPH BY TREVOR JONES

Betting

by Graham Rock

Betting on racehorses is for those who believe that they are masters of their own destiny, a definitive statement that skill, application and discipline can defeat the forces of rationality.

Man has devised many elaborate methods to satisfy the gambling instinct, but none as alluring as racing; blue-blooded thoroughbreds, fleet and beautiful, tested to find the fastest horse, to reward the most perceptive players.

So much is in favour of the bookmaker. The odds are compiled to produce a theoretical profit regardless of the outcome, and while the racehorse is relatively consistent, some results are inexplicable. The enemy chalks up prices for every horse, in every race, on every day. Choice is the sole weapon of the punter.

The needy and the greedy are the traditional mainstays of the betting ring, but neither should indulge. The judgement of those who cannot afford to fail is inevitably distorted, while those who do not care whether they win are almost certain to lose.

Betting on the Tote is effectively backing your own opinion against that of rival punters. Like any speculation it can be profitable, but beating the machine does not offer the same satisfaction as defeating an opponent who defies you to win.

The form book is available to every aspirant; how its pages are interpreted divides the winners from the losers. At least as important as an intelligent interpretation of past results, though, is the successful management of betting stakes.

The psychology of gambling follows a familiar pattern: on a winning streak the punter's instinct seems flawless, a conductor commanding the orchestra of fate with unerring accuracy; but all too often the soaring symphony fades into a melancholy requiem for lost dreams. Objectivity is supplanted by complacency; considered investment degenerates into superficial speculation and as the magic vanishes, the profits ebb away. Exhilaration is followed by depression, an abyss of self-torment from which a rapid recovery seems the only tolerable remedy. The sad chase to recoup begins, with the bookmaker inevitably triumphant.

Novice punters suffer this emotional tempest several times before they are able to bet with equanimity. Along with the losers, winners have to endure the rollercoaster ride of fortune, but the race of experience has taught them how to accommodate the highs and lows. Bold in victory, circumspect in retreat, above all, the successful horseplayer has learned to harness the monster that promises riches or ruin.

Everyone with the hours and the inclination can make a profit. Money is replaceable, but the passing of the years in inescapable, and most of us surrender time in exchange for reward. Consequently, winnings from gambling feel as though they have been gained without due sacrifice, a seemingly effortless revenge on the yoke of employment.

Ego explains why betting is so seductive, and so addictive. Choosing a horse, backing it and watching it surge clear of the field is thrilling; adrenalin courses through the winner, euphoria embraces him, caressing his conceit, confirming his superiority, over the bookmakers, over his fellows, over the system.

Ride the tiger or the horses but beware its razor fangs.

Jerry Bailey wins the Breeders Cup Classic on Black Tie Affair (above).
Trainer Mick Channon beams from the Royal Ascot parade (opposite).

PHOTOGRAPHS BY TREVOR JONES

Chapter Four

Personalities

Champion jockey Tony McCoy shouts with delight celebrating the success of Mr Mulligan in the Gold Cup. Choirboy Walter Swinburn gets a mud treatment for his youthful features.

Tony McCoy wins the Gold Cup on Mr Mulligan, 1997 (left).
Walter Swinburn after Halling's flop in the 1995 Breeders Cup Classic (above).

PHOTOGRAPH BY TREVOR JONES (left)
PHOTOGRAPH BY GEORGE SELWYN (above)

The greatest ? After a short stretch away the Long Fellow returns to racing at Leicester, one of England's less celebrated flat racecourses. Later the unmistakable style takes him to victory in the Breeders Cup Mile on Royal Academy.

Lester returns at Leicester, 1990 (left).
Winning on Royal Academy (above).

PHOTOGRAPHS BY TREVOR JONES

*F*or *he's a jolly good fellow. French trainer, François Doumen leads in The Fellow after triumph in the Cheltenham Gold Cup.*
Jockey Adam Kondrat celebrates amidst the merry-go-round atmosphere of the Cotswolds in March.

Adam Kondrat wins the Gold Cup on The Fellow, 1994.

PHOTOGRAPH BY TREVOR JONES

Legends

by Julian Wilson

I wonder if the perfect racehorse has ever been foaled ?
If so it was Eclipse.

The story of Eclipse, foaled in 1764, is one of the great racing legends. To his great benefit he did not race until the age of five.

He was taken to Epsom racecourse to compete for a £50 plate to be run in three four mile heats. In the first heat he won easily—so much so that in his next heat the legendary gambler Colonel Dennis O'Kelly bet that he could nominate the finishing order of the field of five.

When the bet was accepted O'Kelly stated that his forecast was "Eclipse first, the rest nowhere" meaning Eclipse would finish a distance or about 240 yards in front of his rivals.

O'Kelly won the bet and subsequently acquired the horse.

Eclipse was never beaten, and never extended, in 18 races. His skeleton was reassembled after his death and now stands in the National Horseracing Museum in Newmarket.

His magnificent frame supports the widely held theory that exceptional heart rate was the basis of his remarkable speed and stamina.

So what does make a great racehorse ?

The most important factor is class. It is an attribute manifested by the ability to quicken at any stage of a race. Speed is the essential ingredient for a successful racehorse. It is the common factor in all of the great ones.

There are many very good horses, and very popular horses, who possess outstanding stamina, indomitable courage and in the case of National Hunt horses, breathtaking jumping ability.

But the great horse is the one who has the indefinable quality of "class ", who can find the extra gear, notably at the end of a true run race.

We saw this in Sir Ivor's Derby, in Dancing Brave's Prix de l'Arc de Triomphe and Arkle's famous first Cheltenham Gold Cup.

Of course, greatness has different manifestations in other countries. In America where they race on the hateful 'dirt', galloping is the name of the game. Secretariat displayed his greatness by galloping his classic rivals into a 31 length submission in the Belmont. Secretariat was that day the closest contemporary reincarnation of Eclipse.

The components that create the framework of class are conformation, soundness, athleticism, heart-room, honesty and an appetite for racing.

Several of these qualities are detectable in the sales ring. Many high class horses have five or six of these gifts, but lack the ultimate element. Nothing is more frustrating than to own a racehorse with the perfect engine, but with "wheels" that puncture.

The great horses are like great batsmen. They make a task which lesser mortals would find difficult appear incredibly easy. That's Class.

Those of us who love racing and racehorses dream of the great moments as a gold prospector dreams of the lucky strike. When it happens - the manifestation of greatness - the experience is almost erotic. First, there is an enervating tingle, followed by an overwhelming wave of emotion that leads to tears welling in the eye. I remember vividly the sensation of Secretariat's Belmont. In my embarrassment I was unable to speak for at least a minute!

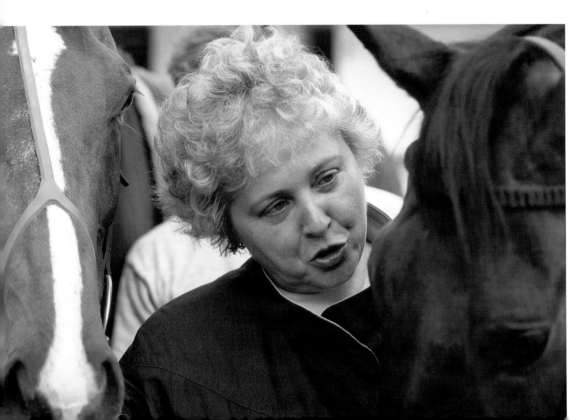

Ladies in waiting. Owner Lady Beaverbrook celebrates with Willie Carson after Minster Son's win in the St Leger. Trainer Jenny Pitman shows compassion for two of her equine companions, as only she can.

Lady Beaverbrook and Willie Carson after the 1988 St Leger (top left).
Trainer Jenny Pitman (bottom left).

Photographs by George Selwyn

The first ladies of the turf. Two of the most knowledgeable in the sport, Her Majesty The Queen at inclement Ascot and her redoubtable mother at Cheltenham with Sirrell Griffiths, owner of the 100/1 winner of the Gold Cup - Nortons Coin.

Her Majesty the Queen Mother & Sirrel Griffiths (above).
Her Majesty the Queen (right).

PHOTOGRAPHS BY GEORGE SELWYN

The height of fashion. Patriotism has gone to the head of one Ascot racegoer. The Tokyo paddock attracts the attentions of a bank of Japanese punters, while from the betting ring at Chester, England, the crowds gather to see a parade of a different kind.

Colourful costume at Royal Ascot (top left).
Japanese crowds zoom in on their favourite (bottom left).
Chester crowds (facing).

PHOTOGRAPHS BY GEORGE SELWYN (top and bottom left)
PHOTOGRAPH BY TREVOR JONES (facing)

The highs and lows of racing life. Aliysa wins the Oaks for owner His Highness the Aga Khan only to be later disqualified, prompting the withdrawal of the Aga's horses from England. On another day the champion Shergar wins the Derby. He met a more tragic fate at the hands of the IRA.

Shergar wins the Derby by a wide margin in 1981 (above).
HH Aga Khan and Aliysa's Oaks victory (right).

PHOTOGRAPH BY GEORGE SELWYN (above)
PHOTOGRAPH BY TREVOR JONES (right)

A crazy cocktail. One wrong move and you're finished - well not quite. Everybody makes mistakes, as the outstanding jockey Kieren Fallon did when riding Bosra Sham in the Eclipse. Eclipsed that day, but Cecil and Fallon look to be a formidable team for the future. Cecil had previously called the fine filly Bosra Sham "his greatest".

Bosra Sham wins the 1996 1000 Guineas (right).
Trainer Henry Cecil (below left).
Jockey Kieren Fallon (below right).

PHOTOGRAPH BY TREVOR JONES (right)
PHOTOGRAPHS BY GEORGE SELWYN (below left and right)

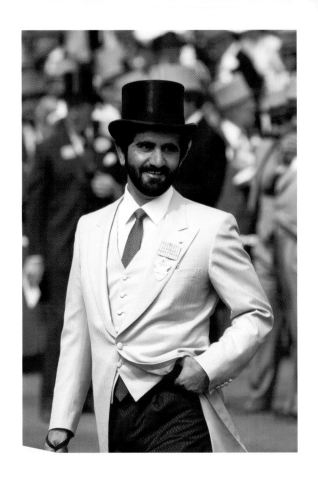

The rough with the smooth. Leading racehorse trainers Peter Chapple-Hyam who works and plays hard and Sir Mark Prescott who, like his top hat also enjoys a busy old life. Meanwhile, the world's leading owner Sheikh Mohammed in relaxed and formal attire.

Trainer Sir Mark Prescott (top left).
Sheikh Mohammed at Tattersalls (top middle).
Sheikh Mohammed at Ascot (top right).
Trainer Peter Chapple-Hyam (right).

PHOTOGRAPHS BY TREVOR JONES **(top right, left and middle)**
PHOTOGRAPH BY GEORGE SELWYN **(right)**

Much of a trainer's life is spent away from the racecourse - hard work, tough knocks and often a heritage in horse racing that reads like a Northern Dancer pedigree.

Trainer David Nicholson (above left).
Trainer Alec Stewart (above right).
Trainer Harry Thompson Jones (below left).
Trainer Fred Winter and Sprowston Boy (below right).

PHOTOGRAPHS BY TREVOR JONES (above left, above right)
PHOTOGRAPHS BY GEORGE SELWYN (below left, below right)

Sir Peter O'Sullevan the voice of racing and master of his craft. Lord Oaksey one of the racing game's truly fine people, together with his racing and brilliant broadcasting companion - ex jockey John Francome.

Sir Peter O'Sullevan at work (left).
John Francome (below left).
Lord Oaksey (below).

PHOTOGRAPHS BY TREVOR JONES

Everyone loves a grey - but especially this one. Desert Orchid, winner of the public's heart as well as the Cheltenham Gold Cup and three King Georges at Kempton Park, not to mention many other races.

Desert Orchid

PHOTOGRAPH BY TREVOR JONES

A bit of muscle and a bit of cheek. It is said that a jockey will do the equivalent of seventy press ups in the final furlong - top jockey Mick Kinane shows the result. A streaker at Aintree shows a good turn of foot.

Streaker at the 1996 Grand National (top right).
Jockey Mick Kinane (bottom right).

PHOTOGRAPHS BY TREVOR JONES

Who loves you baby? Friends and rivals Frankie Dettori and Olivier Peslier, leading European jockeys at play. Meanwhile, Frankie gets on with some mundane chores.

Racing is becoming ever more an international sport. Cash Asmussen and Steve Cauthen, champions of America, subsequently came and conquered Europe.

Frankie Dettori and Olivier Peslier (opposite top left).
Frankie Dettori at home (opposite bottom left).
Jockey Steve Cauthen (opposite top right).
Jockey Cash Asmussen & trainer John Hammond (opposite bottom right).

PHOTOGRAPHS BY GEORGE SELWYN (opposite page bottom left and top right)
PHOTOGRAPHS BY TREVOR JONES (opposite page top left and bottom right)

Brothers in Arms. Brothers Pat and Paul Eddery and twins Richard and Michael Hills show style in the finish at Ascot and Epsom respectively.

Paul & Pat Eddery (above).
Michael & Richard Hills. Or is it the other way round? (facing)

PHOTOGRAPH BY TREVOR JONES(FACING)
PHOTOGRAPH BY GEORGE SELWYN(ABOVE)

Hats off ! Amber Nectar or Black Beauty. Guinness by the gallon at Cheltenham National Hunt Festival and Fosters by the firkin at the Melbourne Cup. Spontaneous fun and lifelong memories will be provided for those who attend either of these two festivals of racing. Rounding off the turf's diversity— racegoers at St Moritz and Epsom.

Pearly Kings and Queens at Epsom (top left).
Fiddler outside the Arkle Bar (top right).
Dressed for the occasion at St Moritz (centre).
Racegoers at the Melbourne Cup (bottom left).
Crowd before the Melbourne Cup (bottom right).

PHOTOGRAPHS BY GEORGE SELWYN

*T*rainer Arthur Moore celebrates Klairon Davis's victory in the 1996 Queen Mother
Champion Chase, as jockey Francis Woods looks on.

Arthur Moore celebrates (above).

PHOTOGRAPH BY TREVOR JONES

*Winners and losers all the year round from
Goodwood's summer hayday to Uttoxeter's winter
birch.*

**Coastal Bluff wins the Stewards Cup at
Goodwood** (above).
Over the water at Uttoxeter (right).

PHOTOGRAPHS BY GEORGE SELWYN

Race Riding

by John Oaksey

National Hunt racing used to be dismissed as "The winter game - for the needy and greedy". It was - and to some extent still is - the poor relation of its prosperous flat racing ancestor.

But never mind. Each man to his taste, and money isn't everything. For many sportsmen the spectacle, spirit and traditions of National Hunt racing mean more than all the stud fees and prize money in the world.

One of those traditions is still that anyone who is able to buy a horse and keep it in training will be allowed to ride the horse himself as an amateur.

If, as in my case, it quickly becomes clear that no one is foolish enough to hire you as a professional jockey the only alternative is getting paid to hang around the racecourse for some other purpose. This, it turns out, is what racing journalists do - so I became one! (partly on account of a broken collar bone. Anyone close enough to a horse to fall off must surely know something) I got a job with the Daily Telegraph. So for twenty happy years I attempted to combine the roles of writing, riding and latterly, "blathering away on TV".

What you needed at that stage even more than money and luck, was a kindly teacher patient enough to put up with your unlimited, (often apparently unforgivable) mistakes. I found mine in a lovely, long suffering jockey-turned-trainer called Bob Turnell.

It was on my second day "riding out" that it took a big hunter called China Clipper about twenty seconds to discover who was in control. Even I knew that when they put you last in a string of twenty you are not supposed to overtake the other nineteen. As I did so, a bend in the misty gallop revealed (not my fault) an unscheduled flock of sheep. They scattered, so did the string - and it was ten exhausting minutes later that China Clipper and I walked back along the Marlborough Road.

Twenty five years old, as bald as I am now and never having earned a penny in my life I was literally crying with shame and fatigue as we entered the yard. If Bob Turnell had issued the rocket which I richly deserved, I honestly do not believe I would have ever ridden again - certainly not on a racehorse. His "Be here tomorrow" remain three of the kindest and most important words I ever heard.

On the Newbury day (1956) of my first ride over fences - on a mare called Pyrene (my first winner a month later), I was far too nervous to notice a 4-year-old called Taxidermist winning the selling hurdle. . . But he was to be, not only the best but by far the most significant horse in my "career".

Against the vehement advice of Brown Jack's trainer, the great Ivor Anthony, ("You're mad girl, mad"), Cath Walwyn bought "Taxi" back at the post-race auction for 170 guineas. In the next two seasons he won eight steeplechases including the Whitbread and Hennessy Gold Cups, in both of which I was lucky enough to ride him.

Among the countless lessons Taxi taught me was never to forget that, when credit for winning is being shared out , nearly all of it belongs to the horse.

One Friday at Cheltenham I rode the somewhat gutless favourite for a minor hurdle race - and, patently "outridden" on the flat, was caught close home by Derek Ancil. If modern whip rules had applied Derek might have been in trouble - but as it was, "Look at that pathetic amateur." they said, "Couldn't ride his way out of a paper bag. . . "

Next day, in mud he hated, Taxidermist came to the last fence of the Hennessy Gold Cup with six horses still in front of him - one of them, Kerstin, apparently home and dry. So when Taxi passed them all, catching poor Kerstin on the line, what did the punters say? "What a brilliant finish that amateur rode".

The difference, of course, was that one horse tried, the other didn't. Anyone could look good on Taxidermist.

Amazingly, down the years, I rode several others, nearly, if not quite as good. Poor Carrickbeg, for instance - only seven when Ayala caught him in the last 50 yards at Aintree. Deserving at least one more chance, Carrickbeg was at least a stone better the following year - but broke down irreparably winning at Sandown.

No, I didn't "get tired before him" in 1963 either. I lost my head - and the National - by asking Carrickbeg to recover too quickly when Out and About fell, costing us six lengths four fences from home. If only I'd sat still and given him time, if only . . . It is too late now for me - but they still allow amateur riders - and no one born in the British Isles who loves riding is entitled to complain at this moment. I was incredibly lucky, I know - but for anyone who wants them badly enough the opportunities still exist. There are not, after all, many weekdays without National Hunt race meetings in this country.

Will Ogilvy ended his poem in honour of steeplechasing with the words . . .

"Tis a Game, beyond gainsaying
Made by the Gods for brave mens' playing . . . "

But you don't have to be all that brave to do something you love. I certainly have not found a thrill to take its place.

the *Spirit of Racing*

Cigar displays his awesome power in a workout on Dubai Sands.

Cigar - early morning exercise.

PHOTOGRAPHS BY TREVOR JONES